Reflections on the Run

100

Meditations on Faith, Growth & Commitment

Reflections *on the* RUN

The Rev. Charles B. Fulton, Jr.

Harold Shaw Publishers
Wheaton, Illinois

ISBN 0-87788-818-3

Cover design by David LaPlaca

Library of Congress Cataloging-in-Publication Data

Fulton, Charles B.
    Reflections on the run : 100 meditations on faith, growth, and commitment / Charles B. Fulton, Jr.
        p. cm.
    Includes indexes.
    ISBN 0-87788-818-3
    1. Faith—Prayer-books and devotions—English. 2. Spiritual formation—Prayer-books and devotions—English. I. Title.
BT771.2.F85 1994
243—dc20
                                                                    94-2810
                                                                         CIP

---

99 98 97 96 95 94

10 9 8 7 6 5 4 3 2 1

*Dedicated to my good friend,
Dorothy Sherman Leech,
of Sarasota, Florida,
who has prayed for me
from my ordination day to this.*

Acknowledgments

These selected readings come from twenty-eight years of priesthood—of reading, observing, listening, and applying what the Lord has shown me. They have come from bumper stickers, specialty columns in magazines, books, commentators, devotionals and private, meditative time with the Lord—which is the wellspring of my spirituality.

Basically, each reading is something the Lord has shown me in reference to a situation, practical application of truth, or an intellectual nugget from someone else.

Most of the material is not original but gathered a piece at a time. To all those who have influenced my life; to the Holy Spirit, who has inspired my life; and to Christ Jesus, who has saved my life, I am grateful and offer the practical insights of these pages.

This book would not have been possible without the able assistance of my wife, Judy, as encourager and proofreader. Additional thanks goes to my faithful secretary, Gail Mosely, who has been invaluable as proofreader, organizer, and liaison to my editor and publisher.

I also wish to thank the many unnamed people to whom I've listened and whose books I have read for providing me with numerous illustrations of truth, some of which I've used in this book.

Foreword

This book is for busy people. It is designed to be read in those odd moments between other things that are clamoring for our attention. Each entry is short and to the point. Probing questions, illuminating illustrations and arresting anecdotes all serve to highlight the truth of God found in the Holy Scriptures. These meditations build a bridge between the eternal and the everyday. Some will inspire, others may challenge, and still others rebuke. I believe the Holy Spirit will bring out the special relevance that is needed by all who read.

Don't spend any more time on this foreword. The best thing to do is to begin to read. Start anywhere, at the beginning of the book, in the middle, or near the end, and allow each entry to bring a shaft of bright light into your day.

Everett (Terry) Fullam

Preface

A young man's tragedy and triumph in the 400-meter race at the 1992 Summer Olympics moved me deeply. Just as Englishman Derek Redmond started the race, he immediately popped a hamstring and collapsed. Such a severe injury is excruciatingly painful and ends a runner's chance of finishing. But Derek Redmond finished that race!

If you were watching television that day, you witnessed an amazing demonstration of love. In tears, Derek got back up on his feet and started hobbling slowly and laboriously toward the finish line. All the other runners finished the race in a few seconds. It looked as though Derek would fall again at any moment. Suddenly, however, a man appeared beside Derek. His father had pushed past the security guards onto the track and reached his son.

The father put his arms around his son and let him cry on his shoulder for a second. Then, with his father supporting him, Derek hobbled to the line, finishing the race.

The way Derek Redmond finished that race stands as a sign of hope for all of us. As we "run the race" of Christian living every day, our wisdom and good works don't make us winners. It is our Father God who gives us victory. He stands beside us at all times and picks us up when we fall. He sent his Son to carry us across the finish line.

I wrote *Reflections on the Run* for Christians like you and me who may be running so fast through the busyness of our lives that we often forget we cannot finish the race on our own strength. Our Father is there beside us to give us strength and support, but we get so preoccupied with our activities we don't even acknowledge his presence. We need reminders and reflective moments to get things into perspective. While we are running, we need to pause to reflect on the Lord's presence in our lives.

The Word of God is living, active and sharper than a two-edged sword. The Lord *is* speaking to you and me today. We must observe what is happening in our lives and hear what he has to say to us about it in the Scripture. May *Reflections on the Run* inspire you to embrace Father God through his Son, Jesus, by the power of the Holy Spirit.

"Let us run with perseverance the race marked out for us. Let us fix our eyes on Jesus, the author and perfecter of our faith."
Hebrews 12:1-2

Human Bridges

United Press International reported a very unusual story concerning a bank official who became a hero. Andrew Parker's family, along with many others, was on a ferry boat sinking in the turbulent English Channel. Between the sinking boat and a channel marker was a six-foot cascade of water, which "was too big for people to jump." In Andrew Parker's words, "I just made sort of a bridge." In a moment of courage, he stretched his six-foot, three-inch frame across the gap to become a human bridge, in order that twenty people might reach safety.

His wife, Eleanor, was the first to try to walk across the human bridge. She said, "I stepped on his back, and I was petrified." All the people made it across. Once across, all of them clung to the small island marker until rescuers could throw a rope. Parker then helped them all climb the rope to safety.

You are a priest forever, in the order of Melchizedek.
Hebrews 7:17

The word *priest* means "bridge builder." The body of Christ is to span the distance between where people are in their humanity and where they need to be in safety with Jesus. The turbulence that we must span is the world, the flesh, and the devil.

Corporately as the body of Christ, and as individuals, we also are called to the priesthood. The New Testament states very clearly that every believer is a priest. So we must ask ourselves, "Are we willing to span the dangerous chasms in order that people may walk across our life to safety?"

Decaffeinated Christianity

Decaffeinated Christianity won't keep you awake at night. Decaffeinated Christianity tastes different from the real thing. Though it has a similar color and aroma, the taste is frequently different. For example, in decaffeinated Christianity, counsel can take the place of repentance. Yes, people may go for counsel and make either temporary or minor adjustments in their behavior, but fail to come to the Lord. Then, the person often forgets the counsel and reverts to old sinful habits. However, in the "real thing," when repentance establishes a right relationship with Christ—possibly supported by counsel—then a person receives new life.

Now that you have purified yourselves by obeying the truth so that you have sincere love for your brothers, love one another deeply, from the heart. For you have been born again, not of perishable seed, but of imperishable, through the living and enduring word of God.
1 Peter 1:22-23

God has called an apostolic church to do old things in new ways and new things in old ways. Decaffeinated Christianity permits a spiritual slumber that says, "Make no changes, do nothing different, keep the peace, enjoy the bland." Our Lord Jesus is saying, "Therefore, if anyone is in Christ, he is a new creation; the old has gone, the new has come!" (2 Cor. 5:17).

Jesus is out to change all of us into his likeness. Decaffeinated Christianity causes us to believe that what the world needs is more education, when in fact the world needs a Savior who can give personal salvation and renewal.

What a Gift!

When our youngest daughter was six years old, she became very ill. Her mother and I were in constant consultation with the doctor, but she dehydrated and her general condition deteriorated rapidly.

I remember gathering her up in my arms. She was feverish and her face was pale—a very sick little girl. We rushed to the hospital, where she was placed in the children's ward, and her mother and I began to keep watch at her bedside.

As I looked at her in the hospital bed, my fatherly heart nearly broke. I wished I were in the bed and that I could take her pain and do the suffering for her. When the nurse came to place a needle in her arm for intravenous feeding, she could not locate the vein. My child was stuck again and again. She flinched and sometimes whimpered. Oh, how I hurt. Generally, I can keep my composure, but I began to feel faint and I finally had to leave the room.

Her health was restored quickly, but the memory of her face, her illness, and her pain remain as vivid as if her hospitalization were only yesterday.

Often I realize that Father God, too, had pain when he looked down on humanity suffering in weakness and sin, only he had no place to turn. He could only turn to himself, and so he did. Father God, when he gave the gift of his Son, Jesus, did for you and me what we can't do for ourselves or our loved ones. He met our needs and covered our weakness within himself.

Thanks be to God for his indescribable gift!
2 Corinthians 9:15

You Can't Live on Baseball

The great Ty Cobb of all-time baseball fame said, "For years I ate baseball, I slept baseball, I talked baseball, I thought baseball, I lived baseball."

He then went on to say, "When you get beyond those years of playing professional baseball, you can't live on baseball."

What did Ty Cobb really mean? No matter how good you are in *whatever*, even if the foundation of your life is baseball, it will pass away. If our foundation of life is tied to family, education, background, reputation, interest, or hobby, our foundation is weak and will pass away. We know very well that a poor foundation cannot support a spiritual home.

So what does Jesus say about being Christian in name only? When behavior matches belief, Jesus becomes our foundation. Today we can be foundational in belief and behavior.

For no one can lay any foundation other than the one already laid, which is Jesus Christ. If any man builds on this foundation using gold, silver, costly stones, wood, hay or straw, his work will be shown for what it is, because the Day will bring it to light. It will be revealed with fire, and the fire will test the quality of each man's work. If what he has built survives, he will receive his reward. If it is burned up, he will suffer loss; he himself will be saved, but only as one escaping through the flames.
1 Corinthians 3:11-15

Receive the Holy Spirit

The Norwegian explorer, Roald Amundsen, discovered both poles—north and south. On one of his trips, Amundsen took a homing pigeon with him. When he had finally reached the top of the world, the North Pole, he opened the pigeon's cage and set it free.

One day his wife, back in Norway, looked out from the doorway of her home and saw the pigeon circling in the sky. Immediately, she knew that this was her husband's way of communicating his love all the way from the North Pole.

There is a striking similarity between this story and the sending of the Holy Spirit. Christ could not remain with us physically, so he sent a dove into our hearts to bear witness to his love.

But I tell you the truth: It is for your good that I am going away. Unless I go away, the Counselor will not come to you.
John 16:7

The gift of the Holy Spirit is himself, with as many varied manifestations as there are people:

There are different kinds of gifts, but the same Spirit. There are different kinds of service, but the same Lord. There are different kinds of working, but the same God works all of them in all men. Now to each one the manifestation of the Spirit is given for the common good.
1 Corinthians 12:4-7

Today, there is a gift waiting for you from Jesus. Go ahead—accept him.

Staking Our Lives

Once, during an Arctic night in 1933, Admiral Richard E. Byrd left his specially equipped hut to take a brisk walk. Before long, he realized that he was out of view of the hut and that his footsteps had become covered with snow.

Had he become completely disoriented, the treacherously cold dark night could have been his doom. So he took the walking stick that he had and drove it into the ground. Then he proceeded to walk in different directions from the stick, never taking his eyes from it. Eventually, through this process, he relocated the hut.

This story has a simple and helpful message for us. If we have wandered so far out into the pitch black darkness of this world and sense that we are lost, we can find our way back to the right path by staking our lives on the Cross. Moreover, we can keep ourselves from getting lost if we routinely orient our lives around the Cross. When we keep our eyes on the Cross, we see Jesus in Spirit and in reality.

Let's imitate the wisdom of the great explorer and stake our lives on the cross of Christ.

My steps have held to your paths;
my feet have not slipped.
Psalm 17:5

Chill Out!

Our grandparents were exposed to about one thousand sensate bombardments per day, and we in our childhood were exposed to about twelve thousand bombardments per day. A sensate bombardment is a heavy exposure to media. The average person today is the victim of twenty-four thousand daily sensate bombardments.

Personality experts tell us that the healthy person can accommodate or deal with approximately twelve thousand such exposures or bombardments. Conclusion: We are in the state of destructive bombardment, and we are under serious attack through our senses.

What is the answer?

You will keep in perfect peace him whose mind is steadfast, because he trusts in you.
Isaiah 26:3

Without a quiet place and some time with Jesus, we can become jaded, frustrated, confused, and manipulated by a secular society. The young people of today have an answer for chaotic behavior and their admonishment comes in this form: "Chill out!"

Jesus is asking us to take stock of our spiritual lives and refuse the confusion of today—administered through inhuman overdoses of sensate stimulation—and accept his peace. Chill out!

Compartmentalized

In his last interview with James Dobson, serial killer Ted Bundy revealed that he had compartmentalized the bizarre wickedness of his multiple murders and had gone on with his life as if nothing had happened.

To some degree, we all behave this way, locking up secret sins in compartments and pretending they are not there so that we don't have to deal with them.

Ted Bundy stated that he was reared in a Christian home. He continued to lived as an all-American boy—the kind who would help to dry dishes and open the car door for you. Bundy was bright, the life of the party, charming, and well-educated. Ted Bundy had kept his murders in one compartment and the rest of his life in other compartments.

This is not so hard to do. In our lives, for example, we compartmentalize our relationships. We may have compartments for the country club, Jesus, the church, the office, our marriage, even our children. There are multiple kinds, shapes, and sizes of compartments in our lives in which we segregate and separate facets of ourselves.

The way to open the windows and doors of the compartments of our lives, in order that Jesus may become Lord of our whole life, is simply to embrace him and to live out the new commandment he has given us.

A new command I give you: Love one another. As I have loved you, so you must love one another.
John 13:34

By giving and receiving the love of Jesus, we become whole persons. We will let the light and the fresh air of the Spirit into our lives when we make ourselves vulnerable by reaching out to others in love.

"You Look Mahvelous!"

Comedian Billy Crystal has built a whole routine around the line, "You look mahvelous, dahling." It is a serious spoof addressing America's preoccupation with outward and superficial appearances.

How "mahvelous" are we? How's my tan? Am I wearing the right sneakers? Have you noticed how slim I have become? Not only am I dressed for success, but my hair is thicker, my eyeliner is thinner, and my new nose job is just right. Come and covet my tight chin, my bosom, and my buttocks, and go ahead and ask me about my diet, my spa, my masseur, my exercise program, my blend of vitamins, and whatever makes me look so mahvelous, dahling.

When we focus on physical and superficial attributes, they become a distraction. Why can't we get below the surface for more spiritual introspection? How is our soul? Why can't we talk about the interior person? The Holy Spirit is yearning for a deeper relationship with us through our spirit.

I pray that out of his glorious riches he may strengthen you with power through his Spirit in your inner being, so that Christ may dwell in your hearts through faith.
Ephesians 3:16-17

Glimpses

We all know that a glimpse is certainly not in any way a vision. However, to me—both spiritually and practically—sometimes a glimpse has been a lifesaving moment.

I think of an incident when Judy (my wife) and I were on a mountain road outside of Cashiers, North Carolina. It was about midnight, the clouds had totally descended onto the road, and there were hairpin turns. We were pulling a horse trailer at eight or ten miles per hour, trying to work our way up the mountain with zero visibility. Between the billows of the clouds, we could occasionally see the white line of the road. There was no place to turn around—actually, no turning back. At that moment, the glimpse of the next ten feet of the white line was more important than a complete vision of the mountain. It was lifesaving.

What do we do when we only have a glimpse of our future and not a vision? First, we don't panic. Second, as we apply good principles of Christian living, so we center ourselves in God's will. It is not necessary to have the whole vision when you have his Word, because you know *his* principles, and you are moving in a faith relationship.

If it hadn't been for glimpses of the center line on the road, we would have lost our lives outside of Cashiers. And without God-given glimpses of himself and our life in Jesus, many of us would frequently be in spiritual jeopardy.

Your word is a lamp to my feet
and a light for my path.
Psalm 119:105

Expect the Best

Arturo Toscanini was one of the greatest conductors of this century. When he was eighty-eight years old, he was invited to conduct the BBC Orchestra at the Great Albert Hall in London. He gave such a spectacular performance that the Board of Trustees of the BBC got together and decided they would invite Toscanini to be the permanent conductor.

The board went to Toscanini and offered to him a two-year contract. It was obvious that Toscanini was very disappointed. His response was, "I was hoping that the contract would not be for two years, but ten years." At age eighty-eight, looking forward to a contract for ten years is a healthy attitude toward life!

Are you excited about today and the next ten years? Do people see in each of us a life that is worth living and a future worth desiring? The way to begin a ten-year plan is to live today in the fullest to the glory of Jesus.

I tell you the truth, anyone who has faith in me will do what I have been doing. He will do even greater things than these, because I am going to the Father. And I will do whatever you ask in my name, so that the Son may bring glory to the Father. You may ask me for anything in my name, and I will do it.
John 14:12-14

The Price Is Right

The world is always asking for money. At the supermarket, the checker never fails to ask you for your money. The bank that holds the mortgage on your house or car never fails to expect a monthly payment. The government insists that there be a withholding from a paycheck to cover Social Security and income taxes, and usually deductions to cover insurance.

Your heavenly Father, however, does not make payroll deductions. There is only one place where there are truly free lunches, and that is in the church. There is never an admission charge. When you are sick, the clergy come any time—day or night. There is free counseling. Our children are baptized and married in the parish without direct costs. Hundreds of people receive newsletters without paying for a subscription.

A funeral home charges for services rendered, but a church is seldom paid at the time of death. Most parishes operate a Sunday school with quality education. There is absolutely no cost or obligation. There are no membership fees, annual dues, and no one will ever know what you contribute except the Lord God. The church is not asking for money—it is asking for *you*, the believer. The Lord Jesus wants far more than your money. He is asking for your heart.

Give generously to him and do so without a grudging heart; then because of this the LORD your God will bless you in all your work and in everything you put your hand to.
Deuteronomy 15:10

Invest in Love

In a classified section in a rather large metropolitan newspaper, the following appeared:

> For sale, one 52-year-old husband. Never remembers anniversaries, birthdays, or special days. Seldom holds hands, hugs, kisses, or says, "I love you." Rarely is kind and tender. Will sell cheap. Two cents. Call 555-0366. Will dicker.

Loving Jesus, your mate, your children, or your neighbor as yourself takes a large personal investment. Those who invest little receive little, and likewise, those who invest well receive great returns.

Scripture teaches that we must love each other with the same unselfishness with which Christ loved the church.

This is a profound mystery—but I am talking about Christ and the church. However, each one of you also must love his wife as he loves himself, and the wife must respect her husband.
Ephesians 5:32-33

Whether it be love of husband or wife, child, or friend, when Jesus stands in the middle of the relationship, it will be priceless.

A Domesticated Goose

Sören Kierkegaard once told this parable about a wild goose that was brought down by a hunter's shot. Fortunately, only the goose's wing was wounded, and he landed in a barnyard. Naturally, the domesticated ducks, geese, and chickens were quite startled by this sudden visitor from the sky. Soon, however, they sidled up to him and asked him to describe what it was like to fly.

The wild goose proceeded to extol the glories of flight, remarking how thrilling it was to soar out in the wild blue yonder. "Why, this barn down here looks like it's only an inch high," he said, "and you all are but specks in the landscape seen from such a distance."

The domestic fowl were quite impressed by his little speech. Some time later, they asked him again to describe the glories of flight. It got to be quite a weekly occasion, while the goose's wing was healing, for him to get up in front of the others and talk. They even provided a little box for him to stand on so they could see him better. What do you think happened? While the domestic fowl very much enjoyed hearing about the glories of flight, they never tried to fly themselves. And the wild goose—even though his wing healed—continued to talk about flying, but he never tried to fly again.

Let us not live in the past, for our salvation and empowerment from Jesus are for today.

Not that I have already obtained all this, or have already been made perfect, but I press on to take hold of that for which Christ Jesus took hold of me.
Philippians 3:12

Time Out!

What if you knew that you only had one year to live? How would you live it, and would there be more time for the Lord? What would be different, and how would your priorities change?

No doctor can tell you at what exact moment anyone will die. Incidentally, no OB/GYN can tell you the exact moment a child will be born. Every father and mother can attest to the fact that it is God's appointed moment.

Sow for yourselves righteousness,
reap the fruit of unfailing love,
and break up your unplowed ground;
for it is time to seek the LORD,
until he comes and showers righteousness on you.
Hosea 10:12

There are some "time outs" in life. These are special moments with Jesus when we especially recognize him as Lord of our life. Are you taking some time outs with him along the way? Special times with Jesus are moments of enrichment and focusing. "Time outs" often help to establish priorities and prepare us for the major challenges of life.

Have you taken a "time out" lately? Do you need some refreshment, and a season of evaluating priorities and refocusing your time and energy? Since we neither know the time or the date that our life will end, will we be prepared at any time because we have had some times like this and are prepared to be with Jesus forever?

In the Blink of an Eye

In the brief time it takes to blink our eyes, another person dies from starvation. The average person blinks his eye thirteen times every minute. Thirteen people starve to death in that same minute.

Meditate on this passage, and for heaven's sake, don't blink the implications away:

For I was hungry and you gave me something to eat, I was thirsty and you gave me something to drink, I was a stranger and you invited me in, I needed clothes and you clothed me, I was sick and you looked after me, I was in prison and you came to visit me. . . . I tell you the truth, whatever you did for one of the least of these brothers of mine, you did for me.
Matthew 25:35-36, 40

During the time that we have reflected on this Scripture, at least two people have died.

Does God care? Who is really going to be held responsible?
. . . Blink . . . Blink . . . Blink . . .

Smitten

A lineman for an electric company was working on a new utility pole that was damp and green. The street was wet. Overhead was a high-voltage line carrying 33,000 volts. The lineman was guiding the pole as it was being swung into place. Suddenly, one of his buddies ran for him and slammed him to the ground.

As the lineman was lying on the ground, he looked up to see that the wet pole had just touched the high-tension wire. But for the sudden slam from his friend, he would have lost his life.

Does God do less to save us? From time to time, the Lord smites us, but we should recognize his intervention.

It was good for me to be afflicted
so that I might learn your decrees.
Psalm 119:71

Sometimes God must smite us to save us. Has the Lord smitten you lately?

You are my hiding place;
you will protect me from trouble
and surround me with songs of deliverance.
Psalm 32:7

What on Earth has Happened?

Consider the initials, *BGW*, which could stand for "Before George Washington" or *AMJ*, which would be "After Michael Jordan." Both sets of initials would speak to special groups of people. Think of the initials, *BCE*, which mean "Before the Common Era," because Jews do not recognize the messiahship of Jesus. However, none of these initials bear the impact of B.C. and A.D.—before and after Jesus Christ, the Son of God.

Christ has come. He visited Planet Earth like a meteor from outer space that struck with such impact that the world has never been the same. His birth was only the beginning. When the very worst could be mustered against him and he was crucified as a common criminal, he continued to change the course of the whole human race. His resurrection has torn the curtain of our sin and has opened to us life everlasting. Jesus came to seek and to save all humankind.

What on earth has happened in *your* life because of Jesus?

I am the Alpha and the Omega, the First and the Last, the Beginning and the End.
Revelation 22:13

Patience

Before the traffic light turns green, the driver in the car behind you honks his horn—*and how do you react?*

The third unrealistic request in an impossible time frame has been made—*and what is your response?*

The children are at each other, Dad's late, dinner is burning—*and what is your attitude?*

Patience is part of the fruit of the Spirit and is spoken of frequently in the Scripture. The patience of each one of us is tried again and again through a variety of difficult situations. How do we undergo the stress of this life without going under?

Frequently, people who have *patience* are the ones who can allow things to be done to them and through them, and yet refrain from having extreme reactions. Our only answer lies in the stability of the Lord Jesus, who gives understanding, and the Holy Spirit, who provides the stamina that we need in times of stress.

St. Paul speaks to us concerning not only survival, but success in life, which is often stressful.

And we pray this in order that you may live a life worthy of the Lord and may please him in every way: bearing fruit in every good work, growing in the knowledge of God, being strengthened with all power according to his glorious might so that you may have great endurance and patience, and joyfully giving thanks to the Father, who has qualified you to share in the inheritance of the saints in the kingdom of light.
Colossians 1:10-12

The closer we draw to the Lord, the more patient we can be. Because of our joy in Jesus, we can walk in patient endurance and truly inherit the blessings of God that have been set aside for us since the foundation of the world.

Watch My Lips

Eccentric former governor of Louisiana, Earl Long, once said of another politician: "You know how you can tell that fellow is lyin'? Watch his lips. If they are movin', he's lyin'."

I cannot think of a more important goal than to "watch our lips." Truth is priceless. Jesus said he is the way, the truth, and the life. Moses reminds us under the anointing of the Holy Spirit in the Ten Commandments that we are not to bear false witness against our neighbor. None of us are good enough to criticize or judge others. Yet we must be able to be trusted. The world must be able to watch our lips and know that they are under control and are lovingly speaking the truth.

Let's watch our lips and set an example in speech, in life, in love, in faith, and in purity.

The LORD detests lying lips,
but he delights in men who are truthful.
Proverbs 12:22

A Parent's Ransom

Hardly a day goes by that we don't hear on the radio, see on television, or read in the newspaper of a kidnapped youngster. We are all too familiar with the anguished looks on the faces of parents as they seek their missing child.

What would you do if your child were abducted? How would you respond to the request of raising $100,000 to ransom your child? Every parent I know would sell his home and car and liquidate any assets to raise the ransom amount.

Imagine yourself liquidating home, car and assets, leaving the money in a phone booth, and finally gaining the release of your child. As you were picking up your child and were so excited and began to hug and kiss that child, how shocking it would be if the child pushed you away and spurned you, and finally said, "Why did you ransom me, anyway? I didn't care whether I was released or not or if I ever came home."

The story may be far-fetched in relationship to you and your child—but how about each of us and our heavenly Father? For you see, God the Father, in his ultimate desire to ransom us from the kidnapper, Satan, gave up his Son for you and me.

By thought, word, or deed today, are you expressing to your loving Father, "Abba, thank you," or does your ungrateful attitude say, "I don't care whether you ransomed me or not, and I don't care whether I ever come home"?

For there is one God and one mediator between God and men, the man Christ Jesus, who gave himself as a ransom for all men—the testimony given in its proper time.
1 Timothy 2:5-6

Plain Pain

Many people strive to find a painless life. However, our Lord Jesus Christ himself suffered excruciating pain, both physically and spiritually. Our understanding of Jesus is incomplete unless we meditate on that deep physical pain he endured as the nails were driven through his hands and feet, or the spiritual pain and darkness as he became sin for all creation.

Each of us understands the pain of denial and rejection we have endured in certain difficult relationships. So did Jesus at the hands of both Peter and Judas. If the perfect God-man walked this way and knew pain, how much more shall we expect varying degrees of pain ourselves?

The results of physical, emotional, or spiritual pain can either be devastating and destructive or show us more clearly our God who truly loves us. Pain can separate us from God; or through it, he can draw us closer to him—it is our choice. We must not deny the pain of today, or by accepting it, allow it to distort life for tomorrow. Simply stated, pain must be met head-on through remedy or endurance and not permitted to derail life and that which God has purposed for us.

I want to know Christ and the power of his resurrection and the fellowship of sharing in his sufferings, becoming like him in his death, and so, somehow, to attain to the resurrection from the dead.
Philippians 3:10-11

Who's Got the Key?

Honey, where are my car keys?"
"Where are my house keys?"
"Where are the office keys?"
These are familiar questions, which at times are asked in panic, frustration, outright anger, and certainly, need. Not long ago, at the closing of a casket, I saw the lid locked down and the key removed and given to a loved one. This was not only a symbol, but it was the last look at a loved one for a season.

My mind couldn't help but turn to the question, "Who's got the key now?"

Easter is the key, but who holds it?

I am the Living One; I was dead, and behold I am alive for ever and ever! And I hold the keys of death and Hades.
Revelation 1:18

Who has the key to death and life? *Jesus!* The One who has the key to every casket is our Easter Jesus. Do you know who has the keys, and where they are? They are with Jesus, and they will be used at the resurrection for every believer.

Since you know where the keys are, have you told everyone you know who holds them?

Lost and Found

One evening, my daughter's wallet was stolen while she was attending a youth meeting. We all understand that not everyone in the church is redeemed and without certain problems. She was very upset about losing her wallet, not so much because of the money, but because of personal identification and other important items—not to mention the cost of the wallet. There was also disappointment in the obvious dishonesty.

I met her in the hallway and saw her tears. As she left, I came before the Lord and asked if he would help me find the wallet. For a moment, there was that awesome silence and then he spoke to me and said, "It's in the trash can by the front door."

It was the only place that I looked, and it was there. How special of God to meet me at my point of need.

Jesus is the Lord of "lost and found." He is the only one who can deal with the lost, from a wallet to a person. He is the only one who can help us continually find our way. Are we too sophisticated to ask for the small things of life? Are our problems too large for the Lord of life, Jesus, to handle?

Remember, Jesus is the Lord of the lost and found.

Are not two sparrows sold for a penny? Yet not one of them will fall to the ground apart from the will of your Father. And even the very hairs of your head are all numbered. So don't be afraid; you are worth more than many sparrows.
Matthew 10:29-31

"It Will Be Different with Me"

In the book, *A View from the Zoo*, former zookeeper Gary Richmond explains that raccoons go through a glandular change at the age of twenty-four months. After this change, they often attack even their owners. Thirty-pound raccoons may attack with the force and fury of one-hundred-pound dogs.

Richmond felt compelled to warn his young friend, Julie, of the change coming to her pet raccoon. Julie listened politely as he explained the approaching danger. She responded by saying what people often say, "It will be different with me." She smiled as she added, "Bandit wouldn't hurt me. He just wouldn't."

Three months later, Julie underwent plastic surgery for facial lacerations sustained after Bandit attacked her for no apparent reason.

No matter what our age, we frequently make the same very dangerous response, "It will be different with me." However, I have interviewed many people hooked on drugs, and never has anyone told me that he expected to become addicted after the very first usage. Persons who become involved in extramarital affairs do not consider beforehand the destruction they can bring to other people involved. The response is always, "It will be different with me."

The Lord is calling us to holiness, righteousness, and a realistic view of the world and ourselves. Be it in the situations mentioned above—or any situation where the individual goes against God's will—he loves the sinner but hates the sin, because he knows the devastation that follows sin.

Make every effort to live in peace with all men and to be holy; without holiness no one will see the Lord.
Hebrews 12:14

Two Different Birds

Over the summer, two different birds have made a special impression upon me. While traveling on a holiday, I noticed a buzzard circling over the road, looking for dead or crippled animals, casualties of modern life.

After reaching my destination in the mountains, I also noticed the hummingbird, who was visiting one blossom after the other, seeking sweet nectar. Both birds found what they were searching for—dead meat or sweet nectar.

So it is with humans. We find what we search for. Those who are looking for dead issues, the casualties of life, and the decadent find them through a critical spirit. Those seeking the lovely, the living, and the sweet find them through the Holy Spirit.

You will always find both "buzzards" and "hummingbirds" in human relationships—in church, in marriage, in business. One person circles in criticism; the other visits in love. One is negative; one is positive. One is a scavenger and the other is lovely and intriguing.

Why do you look at the speck of sawdust in your brother's eye and pay no attention to the plank in your own eye?
Matthew 7:3

Batter Up!

The great Mickey Mantle, who could hit a baseball right-handed or left-handed, had 1,710 strikeouts and 1,734 walks in his career with the New York Yankees.

He came to bat 3,444 times and did not hit the ball. If a man playing regularly in the big leagues usually has 500 at bats per season, then Mickey Mantle played the equivalent of seven years without ever hitting the ball!

Do you feel that sometimes it seems like seven years since you hit the ball?

Examine yourselves to see whether you are in the faith; test your-selves. Do you not realize that Christ Jesus is in you—unless, of course, you fail the test? And I trust that you will discover that we have not failed the test.
2 Corinthians 13:5-6

Having a long list of strikeouts or even walks does not necessarily mean that one has failed. The great Mickey Mantle did not fail the hero's test in the big leagues. You will not fail the test with Father, Son, and Holy Spirit present through your strikeouts and walks, but you will overcome through your hits in faith. Our success rests in our faith and not in our strikeouts or walks. So, today come with faith and step up to the plate.

Junk

Americans create and consume tons of junk. We lead the world in producing garbage and disposable waste. We are the World Champion Junk Food Consumers! We also lead the world in receiving junk mail. The junk mail Americans find in their mailboxes every day, if burned, could produce enough energy to heat 250,000 homes for a year. We receive almost two million tons of junk mail every year, the equivalent of 100 million trees. About 44 percent of all that mail is never even read. Nevertheless, the average American still spends eight full months of his or her life just opening junk mail.

It couldn't be God's purpose for us to be sustained by junk food, to read junk mail, and in the process, live to create junk. The alternative to junk is God's wonderful and holy provision for our life. Ponder these words:

Who may ascend the hill of the LORD?
Who may stand in his holy place?
He who has clean hands and a pure heart,
who does not lift up his soul to an idol
or swear by what is false.
Psalm 24:3-4

God doesn't make junk.

Practical Atheism

For many, the church is a helpmate. The church as a helpmate may offer services for the hungry, the underclothed, and the troubled. She may be considered the baby sitter, the entertainer, the nurturer, the stimulator, the conscience, and the place of meeting.

As the body of Christ, the church may accomplish all the things listed above. However, until she knows the mind and does the will of the body's head, Jesus, she is atheistic. For you see, the primary mission and function of the church is to know the Father in worship and power through Jesus and his Spirit.

There are many who are willing to invest themselves in activities and seek the benefits of the body of Christ, and yet never commit to Jesus, who is the head of that body. Daily personal worship, weekly corporate worship, and powerful ministry is the will and purpose of Jesus to the glory of the Father, enabled by the Holy Spirit. To forget and forsake our mission is to become practical atheists.

Yet a time is coming and has now come when the true worshipers will worship the Father in spirit and truth, for they are the kind of worshipers the Father seeks. God is spirit, and his worshipers must worship in spirit and in truth.
John 4:23-24

Priesthood

Author Alex Haley, researching for his historic book, *Roots*, embarked on the freighter the *African Star* sailing from Monrovia, Liberia, to Jacksonville, Florida. Following dinner for four consecutive nights, he crawled into the cavernous dark hold of the ship, stripped to his underwear, and lay on his back on some broad, thick, rough-sawn timber wedged between sections of cargo to prevent its shifting in the seas. He did this to try more vividly to understand the plight of his ancestors chained so many years before in the bowels of the slave ships. It was not a pleasant voyage. By the third night, he had a miserable cold, and on the fourth night, he abandoned his stay in the hold.

We can only speculate on Christ's agony as he made his way into the world of humanity on Christmas, walked with us as child and man, and bore our sins on the cross as Messiah. Never once did Christ complain, count the cost too high, or discuss his rejection. Never did he give up.

Have you ever placed yourself in someone else's shoes and walked with them for even a short distance in order to minister to them? Do you know the difference between *thinking* kindness and love, and sharing oneself?

But you are a chosen people, a royal priesthood, a holy nation, a people belonging to God, that you may declare the praises of him who called you out of darkness into his wonderful light.
1 Peter 2:9

As Christ shared a common humanity with us, so we should share his godliness in our lives with others. God considers us his priests—willing to identify with others so that we can love them as Jesus loved us.

The Sin of Anxiety

Have you ever noticed that when a child becomes separated in a shopping mall or a large store, he begins to cry and frantically search for his parent?

There is a spiritual lesson to be learned, because quite often, spiritually immature adults do the very same thing. They begin to run from one thing to another, screaming and searching for familiar ground, rather than seeking the Lord.

How can we avoid the sin of unbelief expressed through anxiety, frustration, and lostness? Rather than excuse it, we first need to sit down—and look up.

Be still, and know that I am God;
I will be exalted among the nations,
I will be exalted in the earth.
Psalm 46:10

After we receive our orientation and not only believe but know that God is in control, then we are ready to stand up, lift our heads in confidence, and walk in Jesus' redeeming love.

These are godly solutions for today's troubled times.

Seed for Thought

"Sow a thought, reap an act;
Sow an act, reap a habit;
Sow a habit, reap a character.
Sow a character, reap a destiny."
—Author unknown

There is a sowing and reaping principle that the Bible clearly outlines.

Do not be deceived: God cannot be mocked. A man reaps what he sows. The one who sows to please his sinful nature, from that nature will reap destruction; the one who sows to please the Spirit, from the Spirit will reap eternal life.
Galatians 6:7-8

Increasingly, and in depth, if we sow in sin, we reap sin. What we do sow, we do reap. The Lord Jesus is calling us to reap in righteousness. Righteousness produces righteousness. Jesus is calling us to sow generously in thought, word, and deed. Will you sow for him today in order that you may reap for him tomorrow?

Driving Anger Away

A young mother and her little boy were driving down the street. The little boy asked, "Mommy, why do the idiots only come out when Daddy drives?" Someday the little boy will understand that Daddy's anger says more about Daddy than it does about the quality of other drivers on the road.

The Easter resurrection of Jesus is God's answer to death. It is the answer to the dangerous sin of anger found in that daddy and the poor quality of some drivers on the road. The Resurrection is the ultimate answer to all our shortcomings and all the evil in our situations—even the ultimate evil of death.

Every child's question and every adult's failure can only be understood at the foot of the cross. The realization of the empty tomb in a personal relationship with Jesus is our ultimate answer. Why search any longer for life's answers to your questions, when all are resolved in the truth of Jesus?

At the foot of the cross, mothers are understood, fathers are forgiven, children have their questions answered, and even other drivers are accepted. Jesus' resurrection has daily incomparable life-changing implications, if you love him.

If we have been united with him like this in his death, we will certainly also be united with him in his resurrection.
Romans 6:5

Open and Closed

In the early 1900s, sexuality and related issues were closed as topics for discussion. However, in that era society was open and willing to talk about their Christianity and spiritual values.

We are living through the results of a sexual revolution in which no subjects of sexuality are closed. All are open, including child molestation, incest, pornography, and homosexuality. Christian and spiritual topics have become closed for discussion. This is a serious and wrongful reversal. We should be open with our Christianity and closed about at least some of the sexual topics.

In seeking the Lord Jesus in this whole matter, would he not have us discuss all subjects in a godly context, directed by the Holy Spirit, to the glory of the Father? We ought not make the world's sins our main topic of conversation. We must center on what God's will is for our lives.

The question isn't what is open and what is closed, but how godly are our understanding and our discussions from a Christian perspective.

Let your conversation be always full of grace, seasoned with salt, so that you may know how to answer everyone.
Colossians 4:6

A Change in Order

He is no fool who gives up what he cannot keep to gain what he cannot lose."

These were the words of Jim Elliot, a missionary to Ecuador who was martyred by tribespeople he was trying to evangelize.

All of us must sacrifice much if we are going to embrace eternal values. You don't have to be a missionary to a distant tribe in South America to understand this principle. Assess your life. Is it being spent foolishly? Are you without purpose? Are you chasing temporal things while losing eternal things? If so, a change is in order.

How do you make such a change? The first step is to hold your life up before the Scripture, and where there is a variance, begin with the power of the Holy Spirit to close the gap. The Holy Spirit will crowd out any sin in our life that prevents us from living out eternal values.

This is not simply a decision to change our life, but a willingness to let the Holy Spirit change us to be more like Jesus. Jesus can make a change in us for his eternal purpose. To follow Jesus means that, daily, there is change going on in our lives.

Whoever finds his life will lose it, and whoever loses his life for my sake will find it.
Matthew 10:39

Overnight Relationships

How do you feel about this bumper sticker?

Wanted: A Meaningful Overnight Relationship

The immoral implications of this bumper sticker are plain. Behind the initial "blush" of the message is a deep-seated spiritual problem. An overnight *relationship* with any person is impossible. This is especially true of our relationship with God.

God is not looking for overnight relationships.

Before I formed you in the womb I knew you,
before you were born I set you apart.
Jeremiah 1:5

In the short term or the long term, we become one with anyone we unite ourselves to.

Do you not know that he who unites himself with a prostitute is one
with her in body? For it is said, "The two will become one flesh."
But he who unites himself with the Lord is one with him in spirit.
1 Corinthians 6:16-17

Let us join ourselves with the Lord Jesus in order that the Spirit may manifest himself in a long-term relationship. God's people want neither an overnight relationship with the ungodly nor with the Lord himself, but they seek purity and a long-standing ministry in Jesus.

Double-Life Sin-Drome

At Emory University, a study of six hundred Atlanta area high school seniors and their parents found that parents tended to seriously underestimate their children's drug and alcohol involvement.

Thirty-five percent of the parents said their children had used alcohol in the preceding month, while 67 percent of the students reported that they had consumed alcohol during that month. Three percent of the parents said their children had used marijuana in the past month, but 28 percent of the students had actually used marijuana.

Why this serious miscalculation on the part of the parents? There are many reasons, but for sure, many parents did not know their children very well and had not spent enough time to direct them around the pitfalls of life and into the Savior's presence.

Additionally, many parents are blind to their children's behavior because of their own behavior. How do parents act when they are away from their children? Would children want to follow their parents as role models?

Only be careful, and watch yourselves closely so that you do not forget the things your eyes have seen or let them slip from your heart as long as you live. Teach them to your children and to their children after them. Remember the day you stood before the LORD your God at Horeb, when he said to me, "Assemble the people before me to hear my words so that they may learn to revere me as long as they live in the land and may teach them to their children."
Deuteronomy 4:9-10

We must not only spend time with our children, but set a godly example for them through our words and actions.

Two Minutes

A national study indicates that young people between the ages of twelve and eighteen spend two minutes daily talking directly and personally to their father if they are male, and four minutes daily talking to their mother if they are female.

What a travesty it is to limit our conversations with children to so few minutes. Can you imagine Father God's grief when he sees us neglect a child he gave us as a gift?

How much time do we invest in one-on-one communication and encouragement? In a depersonalized world, we should take very seriously our responsibility as parents to children who need us so deeply. Additionally, this world needs people who are willing to be interested in others.

God cared so much that he sent not simply a message, or even a set of rules—but himself as a human being. Let us give ourselves to others, especially children, as Jesus has given himself to us.

And this is my prayer: that your love may abound more and more in knowledge and depth of insight, so that you may be able to discern what is best and may be pure and blameless until the day of Christ, filled with the fruit of righteousness that comes through Jesus Christ—to the glory and praise of God.
Philippians 1:9-11

911

The 911 emergency system immediately connects us with a dispatcher. On the dispatcher's monitor is displayed the caller's telephone number, address, and name. Even if the caller cannot state what the problem is because of panic and crisis, the dispatcher can send help immediately.

There come times in our lives when, in desperation and pain, we dial 911 prayers. Sometimes we are hysterical, depressed, speechless, panicky, or in extreme pain. We don't know the words to speak, but God hears. Jesus knows our name, our circumstance, and his help is on the way.

Call to me and I will answer you and tell you great and unsearchable things you do not know.
Jeremiah 33:3

God is our refuge and strength,
an ever-present help in trouble.
Psalm 46:1

Old-Fashioned Honesty

Who do you know that best exemplifies old-fashioned honesty? How do our friends, neighbors and associates exemplify honesty? If they don't, where is their failure? Is it in deceptions, misrepresentations, exaggerations, or falsifications?

The way to measure old-fashioned honesty is by a person's actions and conversations. Jesus accused the very religious people of being whitewashed tombs on the outside and rotten on the inside. What a horrible thought—that we are not what we appear to be. It is one thing to have this charge leveled at others, but it is much more shocking when it's directed at us.

True integrity and honesty are outgrowths of a deep relationship with Jesus. We love him so much that we would never want to disappoint him by deceiving or misleading another person.

A lifetime of honesty begins with a period of intensive self-examination.

Righteousness guards the man of integrity, but wickedness overthrows the sinner.
Proverbs 13:6

Calling All Parents and Children

According to a survey, 66 percent of all Americans feel that parents should be free to live their own lives, even if it means spending less time with their children. No wonder we have bumper stickers that say, "It's 10:00 P.M. Do you know where your parents are?"

Jesus spoke of the great love we show in laying down our lives for our friends (John 15:13). Certainly, our children are more precious to us than even our friends. Take time for your child today, not only to please Jesus but to bless your child.

This is a message for children, too. Children, do you have time for your parents? There is not a parent alive, at any age, that doesn't need to know the love of a child. Think of Jesus' response to his Father, even at the desperate scene of his travail in Gethsemane.

Father, the time has come. Glorify your Son, that your Son may glorify you.
John 17:1

I have brought you glory on earth by completing the work you gave me to do.
John 17:4

Look to Jesus for God's answer for parents and children.

He will turn the hearts of the fathers to their children, and the hearts of the children to their fathers; or else I will come and strike the land with a curse.
Malachi 4:6

Drugs and Alcohol

As far as the drug business, I mean, everybody in rock 'n' roll does drugs," says Kevin Dubrow of Quiet Riot.

The other side of the story is that God's people have been filled with the Holy Spirit as far back as the days of the Old Testament.

And I have filled him with the Spirit of God.
Exodus 31:3

Do not get drunk on wine, which leads to debauchery. Instead, be filled with the Spirit.
Ephesians 5:18

Unfortunately, we are not simply talking about wine or beer or even drugs. Every active decision is *for* one thing and *against* another. To choose drugs and alcohol is to choose against God. To choose Father God and Jesus Christ through the power of the Holy Spirit is to choose against addiction and abuse. Everyone is going to be filled with something. The question is this: what will we fill ourselves with?

Elijah went before the people and said, "How long will you waver between two opinions? If the LORD is God, follow him; but if Baal is God, follow him."
1 Kings 18:21

Scars, Signs, and Saints

St. Thomas was the last of the eleven to see the risen Christ. Thomas was not a man to hazard his life and commitment on a false report, mistake, hallucination, or fabrication.

Unless I see the nail marks in his hands and put my finger where the nails were, and put my hand into his side, I will not believe it.
John 20:25

The scars on Jesus' body—the signs for the doubter of the Lord's compassion—and his commitment of his whole life produced the saint. Scripture says that all have fallen short of the glory of God. So in our sin of doubt and failure, only the grace of Jesus makes sainthood possible.

Christ's crucifixion scars and his shed blood speak of the depth of his love and care. His Word is a light to our feet, his Spirit is our strength, his love is our inspiration, his resurrection is our faith, and ruling and reigning with him is our hope.

Scars, signs, and saints all have their place in our spiritual growth. Have you forgotten the scars, the signs, or his saints? Where are you today with Jesus?

Through it all, Jesus is calling us to himself.

Saint, will you come?

The Creator

America has gone from pantheism to pan-atheism. A pantheist is one who believes that God is in everything. On the other hand, the pan-atheist sees God in nothing.

A pantheist says that God is in a rock, God is in a tree, God is in the sunrise, God is in the sunset. It is true that his creation expresses him, but God is not simply or totally present under the guise of a rock, cloud, tree, sunrise, or sunset.

A pan-atheist talks about Mother Nature, luck, coincidence, and God as an outside force, rather than as Father, Son, and Holy Spirit.

The Lord would have us see him in all things as God the Father, the Creator; God the Son, Redeemer; and God the Holy Spirit, Sanctifier.

The earth is the LORD's, and everything in it,
the world, and all who live in it;
for he founded it upon the seas
and established it upon the waters.
Psalm 24:1-2

Garbage In—Garbage Out!

When computers spew forth false information, technicians pinpoint the cause as "garbage in, garbage out."

Unless we discipline ourselves to heed some very important Scriptural counsel, "garbage in, garbage out" is also a true-to-life description of our minds and behavior.

Finally, brothers, whatever is true, whatever is noble, whatever is right, whatever is pure, whatever is lovely, whatever is admirable— if anything is excellent or praiseworthy—think about such things.
Philippians 4:8

These words of Paul the apostle are our answer to the "garbage in, garbage out" problem. Either our lives will be just that, or they can be measured by what is true, noble, right, pure, lovely, and admirable. Make no mistake. There is an answer to every situation, and it doesn't have to be "garbage in, garbage out."

But seek first his kingdom and his righteousness, and all these things will be given to you as well.
Matthew 6:33

So why deal in garbage?

Tattooed

Erwin Lutzer, pastor of the Moody Church in Chicago, tells about a woman who had had an abusive and alcoholic boyfriend. The boyfriend had insisted on placing a tattoo on her arm. She finally acquiesced and was tattooed.

The woman is now very happily married to someone else, but she still has the tattoo. More significant than the tattoo is the fact that her mind daily revisits the memory of her pain, that boyfriend, and all that went with that relationship.

Not everyone's tattoo is on his or her arm. Many of us have deeply embedded emotional tattoos, causing great spiritual discomfort. Like the woman, each of us must be able to find a way around our painful and sinful past. Jesus can heal your memory and remove your tattoos.

But one thing I do: Forgetting what is behind and straining toward what is ahead, I press on toward the goal to win the prize for which God has called me heavenward in Christ Jesus.
Philippians 3:13-14

When we are seeking Jesus and pressing on, the tattoos of our past fade in the brightness of our faith and love for Jesus and what he is doing for us today.

Don't Shoot the Saints

In 1690, the British fought the French for the control of the St. Lawrence River. The British commander ordered Admiral Phipps to take eleven ships and anchor outside Quebec and wait for the British land forces before starting the naval assault.

Admiral Phipps arrived early and saw statues of the saints on the roof of Quebec's Roman Catholic Cathedral. He spent some time firing at those statues for target practice with the ship's guns. When the land forces arrived for the joint assault, Phipps was running low on cannon balls. He had used his ammunition to shoot at the saints!

There are many well-intentioned, well-trained, and highly motivated Christians who spend their time verbally shooting at the saints. Is your verbal activity an encouragement to the saints, or is it an assassination? Don't shoot at the saints!

The words of a gossip are like choice morsels;
they go down to a man's inmost parts.
Proverbs 18:8

Recognized

A farmer in Ohio was approached for a job by a young man named Jamie. Jamie became an excellent employee for Mr. Taylor, the farmer. After some months, Jamie came to Taylor and said that he and the wealthy man's daughter had fallen in love, and he was asking the father for his daughter's hand in marriage.

Taylor was incensed. He said that he had treated Jamie well. Was this to be his repayment? So, Jamie left. Many years later, when Taylor was in the barn, he found where Jamie had carved his name. It read, "James A. Garfield," who subsequently became General and President Garfield.

The farmer, who could have been the father-in-law of the president of the United States, had failed to recognize many years before the real value of Jamie Garfield.

There is One of unparalleled value who stands ready to recognize your worth. To recognize the value of Jesus is to call him not only Savior, but Lord. Certainly, he is our personal Savior from sin and separation, but he is also Lord of our lives. He recognized us by giving all he had for us. Furthermore, he wants to dwell in us and make us his brother or sister in the family of God—forever.

Whoever acknowledges me before men, I will also acknowledge him before my Father in heaven.
Matthew 10:32

Dropping Your Guard

Are you open to scrutiny, or do you hold yourself above questioning?

You can place a protective shield about yourself that says, "Don't question me; I am the total authority about myself." By our unapproachable attitude we can say to other people and even to God, "Don't bother me."

Why not let down your guard, drop your shield, and expose your motives by comparing them to the will of God? Important and appropriate questions like these should be asked: What is the reason behind our actions? Why do we say yes or no? What is the motive for writing that letter? Why are we excited over this opportunity? What causes us to bring up this subject?

Truthful answers to questions like these will always reveal our motive, and our motive expresses the reason for our commitment. Ultimately, we are accountable to God for all that we think, say, and do, no matter what surface impression we may convey to others.

The word of God is living and active. Sharper than any double-edged sword, it penetrates even to dividing soul and spirit, joints and marrow; it judges the thoughts and attitudes of the heart. Nothing in all creation is hidden from God's sight. Everything is uncovered and laid bare before the eyes of him to whom we must give account.
Hebrews 4:12-13

Seeking God

Many people live as though they are caught between the *secular* and the *sacred*. They perceive a wide difference between the worldly and the holy. This reality shows itself in their thinking and in their behavior.

For instance, they regard Bible reading, prayer, and praising God as worthy to be called sacred. However, they see washing dishes, mowing the yard, and helping one's neighbor as secular activities.

Through Scripture, we know that Jesus lived in the physical world and did all things to the glory of God. Jesus can easily be pictured assisting his father, Joseph, around the carpenter shop. Likewise, we can picture him as our Savior on the cross. Both of these situations are sacred because he did them both to his Father's glory.

If there are areas in our life that cannot be considered sacred, it could be because they are areas of sin, or because we have not put God first in those areas. We should frequently examine our thoughts and actions against a spiritual yardstick. If there is more secular than sacred in our life, or if there is a definite spiritual dividing line, it is time to refocus and fervently seek God and his will for us.

So whether you eat or drink or whatever you do, do it all for the glory of God.
1 Corinthians 10:31

Double-edged Razor

Perhaps no cutting tool is more dangerous than a double-edged razor. It has the potential to cut in several directions and must be handled with extreme care.

Sin can be like a double-edged razor blade. For example, there is a two-edged sin in wrongful self-evaluation. One edge is the sin of pride, which occurs when people think too highly of themselves. The other edge of the same razor is the sin of despair. Despair produces a broken relationship with God just as easily as does the sin of pride. Whereas pride is an exaggerated trust in oneself, so despair is a distrust of self and, ultimately, of God.

Be very careful. The double-edged blades of sin can cause great hurt. False pride and personal despair are equally dangerous. The Lord's amazing grace can handle either sin. Jesus brings us balance, equipping us with humility to dispel pride and confidence to conquer despair.

Trust in the LORD with all your heart
and lean not on your own understanding;
in all your ways acknowledge him,
and he will make your paths straight.
Proverbs 3:5-6

Getting Even

A popular bumper sticker reads, "Don't get mad, get even."
Yet revenge can be very hazardous to our health. A Greek
legend tells about an Olympic athlete who begrudged the
public acclaim given to his victorious competitor. The athlete
seethed with anger when a statue was erected for the new
Olympic champion.

Nothing would do but that he seek his own idea of revenge,
which was to destroy the statue. Each night he secretly chis-
eled away at the foundation; he knew that the statue would
eventually topple. The envious and disgruntled athlete succeeded all too well—the statue fell and killed him with the
chisel in his hand!

What are the high costs of getting even?

Anger, envy, jealousy, and revenge are toxic to spiritual
health. Those who indulge in them will not inherit the kingdom of God.

*But the fruit of the Spirit is love, joy, peace, patience, kindness,
goodness, faithfulness, gentleness and self-control.*
Galatians 5:22-23

*Bear with each other and forgive whatever grievances you may have
against one another. Forgive as the Lord forgave you.*
Colossians 3:13

Disarm your enemies. Get even by laying down your life
as Jesus did for us all.

Small Group Protection

Musk oxen are very unique animals. When there is a threat to one of their babies, both the mother and the father join together to protect it. Furthermore, every member of the herd encircles the baby to defend it.

Musk oxen are an object lesson for Christians. Will Christian parents fight to protect their young from anything that might hurt or destroy them? Do Christians band together as the mature musk oxen do for the common good and to protect the future generations? Are Christians grouped together for mutual spiritual defense?

We must work two by two and in communities, as did the early church, to protect the young and ensure our future.

Let us not give up meeting together, as some are in the habit of doing, but let us encourage one another—and all the more as you see the Day approaching.
Hebrews 10:25

The Walls of Fear

Toward the close of the century the unbelievable happened. The Berlin Wall crumbled and is now merely a line of rubble. Many can still visualize the East German guards and their attack dogs. These memories will live for a long time to come. What is *not known* is that out of the sixty-five hundred guard dogs that were used on the Wall, only one thousand were actually trained to attack. The other fifty-five hundred guard dogs were suitable as pets, and that is what each and every one has become. No one knew which dogs were vicious and which were not. So, they were all considered dangerous—a tremendously feared symbol of the Wall and enslavement.

The things we often fear are truly unworthy of our concern. Fear gobbles up spiritual energy and misdirects our lives. We must come to understand that there is no fear in love, but "perfect love drives out fear" (1 John 4:18).

Jesus said, "But take heart! I have overcome the world" (John 16:33). He not only has overcome the world, he has overcome death. His proclamation to one who inquired about faith:

I am the resurrection and the life. He who believes in me will live, even though he dies; and whoever lives and believes in me will never die. Do you believe this?
John 11:25-26

To draw close to Jesus is to discern God's will in all things and not to be overcome by earthly fears.
Alleluia, Christ is risen.
The Lord is risen indeed. Alleluia.

Today

A shiny moving van was standing in the front of a beautiful suburban home. The homeowners—husband, wife, and two children—were busy tidying up the front yard when a woman who lived at the other end of the block approached them. She smiled and said sweetly, "Welcome to our neighborhood. Here is a fresh pie I have made to help welcome you to our street and invite you to our church."

The couple exchanged glances with one another in awkward embarrassment. After a few nervous moments, the wife spoke up. "I don't know quite how to say this, but we have been living here for almost two years. You see, we are not moving in. We are moving away."

It is sad to miss an opportunity to minister, but it is more serious to continually miss God's will and purpose over a lifetime that begins today.

The Scripture powerfully uses the word *today*. Some things need to take spiritual precedence. Have you neglected your spiritual priorities, as we all have from time to time? Today is the day to take inventory and stop putting off those spiritual matters that are most important.

Tomorrow may be too late, for the opportunity is given today.

For he says,
"In the time of my favor I heard you,
and in the day of salvation I helped you."
I tell you, now is the time of God's favor, now is the day of salvation.
2 Corinthians 6:2

Real Freedom

Abraham Lincoln went to the slave block. He saw there a girl being auctioned, and he immediately purchased her. When she was brought to him, he said, "Young lady, you are free."

She said, "Please, sir, what does that mean?"

He said, "It means, you are free."

"Does that mean," she asked, "that I can say whatever I want to say?"

Lincoln said, "Yes, my dear, you can say whatever you want to say and go wherever you want to go."

With tears streaming down her face, she said, "Then, what I want to say is that I want to go with you."

When the Holy Spirit comes upon us and sets us free, out of love, we want to follow and be near Jesus and say those things that he would have us say.

The Lord is the Spirit, and where the Spirit of the Lord is, there is freedom.
2 Corinthians 3:17

Concealed Truth

When Karen Morris of Henniker, New Hampshire, was about to graduate from high school, she revealed a startling fact. She could neither read nor write.

It must be noted that Karen was a member of the National Honor Society, was listed in *Who's Who in American High Schools*, and was class president and student council president. Karen, a severe dyslexic, was known as a superb orator and a model student. Over twelve years of school, she had developed such a system of covering up that no one knew she could not even read street signs. She expended great amounts of energy concealing the truth, and she became a slave to her false image.

Many people play a similar game in their relationship with God. They cover up hidden sins that prevent a real relationship with the Lord Jesus. Embedded deeply in their spiritual activities is a false religiosity. Karen had no possibility of learning to read until she dismantled the game she was playing and asked for help. Likewise, it is impossible for us to grow spiritually until we become honest with God and truthful to self.

If we claim to be without sin, we deceive ourselves and the truth is not in us. If we confess our sins, he is faithful and just and will forgive us our sins and purify us from all unrighteousness.
1 John 1:8-9

Living the Vision

At the timberline of Mt. Shasta in California grows the Shasta fir. It spends its early life under the heavy snowpack, which often reaches twenty feet during the winter months. This snow batters and presses the young plant so that it twists and turns and struggles to survive. Then comes a winter when the tree is able to break through the snowpack. It has grown through adversity and then starts to grow like an arrow skyward. Once the victory over the snow has been accomplished, the straightness of this tree is unmatched by any other tree in the region. In the summer, you can see the gnarled and misshapen lower part of the tree. But the straight vertical growth is visible year-round.

So it is with us. No matter what our past and early beginnings are like, when we come to Jesus, there is a total change. We can overcome great obstacles, if we persevere.

What is it like to persevere in Christ? It means that we begin and end each day by dedicating our lives to him. We look and compare each thing that we do on a moment-by-moment basis to the plumb line of Christ's presence in our lives. This is called Spirit-filled living.

Living the vision of Christ takes strong perseverance. Neither successes nor failures make the difference, but our love for Christ does. Nothing in our past, present, or future can truly separate us from Christ, if we are willing to persevere in faith.

May the Lord direct your hearts into God's love and Christ's perseverance.
2 Thessalonians 3:5

Home Sweet Home

A *fugitive* is one who is running away from home.

A *vagabond* is one who has no home.

A *stranger* is one who is away from home.

A *pilgrim* is one who is on his way home.

Although we as Christians are making our way home to God, we innately search for that earthly home, or place of belonging—spiritually, emotionally, and physically. Whether child or parent, we all desire a family home. Additionally, the church should be more of a home as the seasons go by and the years increase. It takes a few Christmases, a few Easters, a few receptions of new members, a few baptisms, and a few memorial services before a sanctuary becomes precious, more of a home. This is what should be happening week by week.

Finally, we come *from* Christ, we live *in* him, we return *to* him, and when that entire circuit is completed, we are *home. Home.* All the way home. There is only one way home, and that's through Jesus, with intermediate stops in our family home and spiritual home.

If you make the Most High your dwelling—
even the LORD, who is my refuge—
then no harm will befall you,
no disaster will come near your tent.
Psalm 91:9-10

Screaming for Life

An abortionist in Sweden got the shock of his life when a ten-week-old baby he was aborting screamed. Air bubbles can occur during an abortion, and a baby of that age has functional vocal cords. All that was needed was for a bubble to locate over the baby's mouth during the abortionist's procedure. Dr. Mats Waktel declared, "I won't perform another abortion as long as I live. And I'll never forget that scream."

For you created my inmost being;
you knit me together in my mother's womb.
Psalm 139:13

Life begins at conception, but God's purposes for each human being ever born are eternal. Pray today for the living, both born and unborn. Pray that each of us will seek God's will and purpose and not a path of convenience and irresponsibility.

A Cure for Fear

Many of us are afraid of big dogs—or unknown dogs; it is a common fear. However, the great scientist, Louis Pasteur, was far more frightened of dogs than most. Even a distant bark would terrify him, because he would flash back to a boyhood memory of a wolf that raced through a village, bringing agony and death to many of his neighbors. Pasteur said, "I have always been haunted by the cries of the victims." Yet in 1882, at the age of sixty, Pasteur gave up all of his other studies in an intense search for the cure for rabies.

For three years, in spite of his deep-seated fears, he risked his life to live with mad dogs. At long last he developed a vaccine to cure the victims of rabies. On a July night in 1885, he tried the first injection on a little boy whose life was doomed. The boy lived.

For God did not give us a spirit of timidity, but a spirit of power, of love and of self-discipline.
2 Timothy 1:7

Louis Pasteur loved humanity in such a way that his God-given love overcame his fears. God's perfect love in all of us can drive out any and all fears.

Doers

A respectable lawyer in Albert Camus' novel *The Fall* is walking along the streets of Amsterdam one night and hears a cry. A woman had fallen into the canal and was crying for help. The lawyer's immediate thought was, *I must help.* But how could a respectable lawyer get involved in this way? What would the implications be? What about the personal danger? After all, who knows what is going on, and what would be the fallout?

By the time he had thought it through, it was too late. The woman had drowned. The lawyer moved on, making all kinds of excuses to himself to justify his failure to act. Camus wrote, "He did not answer the cry for help. This is the man he was."

Jesus ignored bodily danger and assaults on his personal reputation to come to the aid of all humanity as he answered our cry for help. This is the man he was.

What type of Christian man, woman, or child are you?

Not everyone who says to me, "Lord, Lord," will enter the kingdom of heaven, but only he who does the will of my Father who is in heaven.
Matthew 7:21

Finishing the Race

The cheetah runs down its prey on the African plains. The big cat can sprint seventy miles per hour. However, the cheetah cannot sustain the pace for a long distance. Within the long, sleek body of the cheetah is a disproportionately small heart, which causes the cheetah to tire quickly. Unless the cheetah catches its prey in its first flurry, it must abandon the chase.

Some Christians seem to have the cheetah's approach to the Christian life and ministry. They speed into projects with great energy, but lack the heart to sustain the effort. Frequently, the church has the ignominious reputation of fizzling before she finishes. Often people are called on to start harder and run faster, when God's real will and purpose for us is not more speed, but more staying power, which requires a bigger heart. Activity, busyness, and bursts of speed yield nothing unless we allow God to give us a larger heart for him.

Therefore, since we are surrounded by such a great cloud of witnesses, let us throw off everything that hinders and the sin that so easily entangles, and let us run with perseverance the race marked out for us.
Hebrews 12:1

Tossed Salad

No matter what our age, we are all under some form of society's pressure to conform. The standard social solicitation to compliance is, "Everyone's doing it." Frequently, parents come and talk to me about their teenagers who are pleading to frequent places of poor reputation and see R-rated movies. Sometimes husbands or wives come to me, asking advice on how to help a partner who is addicted to pornography. The evils of this world can encroach upon all of us.

I remember vividly conversations with our children about books and other materials unsuitable for consumption. At times when I was holding the line, I thought about how shocked the children would be if we were preparing vegetables for a tossed salad and we also threw in the peelings and stems. The children would want to remove the scraps or would have nothing to do with a salad they considered to be contaminated.

However, many people are willing to pollute their spiritual diet by ingesting pornographic peelings, lewd scraps, and garbage.

If a tossed salad that contains garbage is unappealing to you, then be careful what you eat. If you have spiritual indigestion and a poor testimony, maybe it is because you have tossed too much garbage into your salad.

For the grace of God that brings salvation has appeared to all men. It teaches us to say "No" to ungodliness and worldly passions, and to live self-controlled, upright and godly lives in this present age, while we wait for the blessed hope—the glorious appearing of our great God and Savior, Jesus Christ, who gave himself for us to redeem us from all wickedness and to purify for himself a people that are his very own, eager to do what is good.
Titus 2:11-14

Ethics for America

A Big 8 accounting firm recently published a survey on ethics in American business. Of the more than one thousand executives, deans of business schools, and members of Congress who participated:

- 94% said they felt the business community is troubled by ethical problems today.

- 63% said they believed that a business actually strengthens its competitive position by maintaining high ethical standards.

- 73% attributed relatively high ethical standards that prevail in countries such as the United States more to cultural heritage than to factors such as education and economic conditions.

The cultural factor referred to in the survey is a Christian foundation. America was originally founded upon a Christian vision with Christian purposes. Those who walk closely with Jesus manifest godly ethics. The further we get away from that vision and purpose, the less ethical we are. The question, "Will America ever again assume the position of world leadership?" will be answered in fact by her commitment to Jesus of Nazareth.

Make level paths for your feet
and take only ways that are firm.
Do not swerve to the right or the left;
keep your foot from evil.
Proverbs 4:26-27

Somebody's Wallace

Two women relatives of General Lew Wallace came to the White House when Lincoln was president, asking about the general. He had been involved in a vicious Civil War battle, and they wanted to make sure he had survived. After learning he was alive and well, they spoke rather glibly of their gladness. There had been a casualty named Wallace in the battle, but they were thankful that it was not "our Wallace."

Abraham Lincoln responded soberly, "Yes, but it was somebody's Wallace, wasn't it?"

Love can often be so petty and so self-centered. If our love is not stronger than the world's love, of what value is our Christian faith?

The Scripture poses an important question: if we only love those who love us, what good is our love? Jesus gave us a command to love one another as he has loved us. The church is called to love not only those who are faithful and part of our Christian family, but those who are not—even to the extent of loving those who are known enemies of Jesus and his church. Somebody's child needs love today. Will you give it?

This is how we know what love is: Jesus Christ laid down his life for us. And we ought to lay down our lives for our brothers.
1 John 3:16

True Peace

They will beat their swords into plowshares
and their spears into pruning hooks.
Nation will not take up sword against nation,
nor will they train for war anymore.
Micah 4:3

A text out of context can be a pretext. Pacifists throughout all ages have decided that the above passage of Scripture is an answer to world conflict and wars. However, they do not read the next verses as a foundation for peace. These Old Testament verses indicate that a prerequisite to peace is many nations coming into the presence of the Lord. Also, the New Testament indicates that as nations come to Christ there is peace. Where there is no Christ Jesus, there is no peace.

We must read the whole text and perceive through the eyes of the Holy Spirit what God the Father has for us who follow his Son.

How can we hasten the fulfillment of these prophetic words? How can we bring the nations to the Lord and the church? The "nations" start with the people next to us—next door, next office, next aisle, and next pew. By our word and example we can spread the gospel of peace.

To Tell the Truth!

James Patterson, chairman of J. Walter Thompson advertising agency, says, "People say what others want to hear."

- 91% of people in the United States say they lie routinely
- 36% confess to lying about major matters
- 86% lie regularly to parents
- 75% lie to friends
- 73% lie to siblings
- 69% lie to spouses
- 81% lie about their feelings
- 43% lie about their income

Now for the truth. The Bible says:

LORD, who may dwell in your sanctuary?
Who may live on your holy hill?
He whose walk is blameless
and who does what is righteous,
who speaks the truth from his heart.
Psalm 15:1-2

Truthful lips endure forever,
but a lying tongue lasts only a moment.
Proverbs 12:19

Then you will know the truth, and the truth will set you free.
John 8:32

Don't make yourself a slave to lies. Walk in true freedom in the light of Jesus and his truth.

Sticks and Stones

Sticks and stones can break my bones, but words will never hurt me!"

Following our parents' advice, most of us have tried to use this stoic principle to defend ourselves from verbal attack. It rarely works.

Sometimes the breaking of bones hurts less than a bloodless verbal assault that causes emotional wounds. Quick, careless, or even intentional words slaughter more souls than guns, knives, or all automobile accidents combined.

We have emergency rooms available for those who are physically bleeding, but frequently we walk away from the verbal accident scene and leave the wounded to carry the hurt and pain, sometimes for the rest of their lives. A physical wound usually heals with time and care. However, the wounded human soul normally requires much more for healing and restoration.

Be very careful with that most dangerous weapon of murder—or instrument of ministry—known as the tongue.

Set a guard over my mouth, O LORD;
keep watch over the door of my lips.
Psalm 141:3

Faith

Faith without obedience is not faith.
Faith without service is not faith.
Faith without submission to the Word of God is not faith.
Faith without trust in Jesus is not faith.
Faith without power is not faith.
Faith without righteousness is not faith.

Now faith is being sure of what we hope for and certain of what we do not see.
Hebrews 11:1

Faith is walking hand in hand with Jesus all the way into eternity.

Band-Aids Cannot Heal

Some people eat to relieve depression. Food, however, usually doesn't solve the problem of repressed anger or other emotional difficulties. Nor does it help us cope with an unconscious desire to get vengeance on self or others. It's like thinking a Band-Aid will heal an infection, instead of seeking the needed medical attention. If left unattended, an infection could get worse.

Holding a grudge against self, others, or God is a sin. It is also a serious emotional and spiritual problem that can be expressed physically. Have you ever considered that anger can cause laziness and deep lethargy? There are two natural chemicals in our body which actually cause us to think (serotonin and norepinephrine), both of which are depleted in our brain cells when we become angry and unforgiving. These are the chemicals that travel across the synapses from one cell to the next and cause us to think and move.

A fool gives full vent to his anger,
but a wise man keeps himself under control.
Proverbs 29:11

Expression of our anger through overeating might, at the moment, seem to be a way to solve our problems. But, as is so often true, we try to deal with the symptoms rather than the cause. Band-Aids cannot heal.

Overheard?

Two young boys were overheard discussing a venture that would be disapproved by their fathers. The younger of the two, under great pressure, decided not to participate. The older boy asked him, "Are you afraid that your dad will find out and hurt you?" The response came, "No, I am afraid he will find out, and it will hurt *him*."

Knowing our heavenly Father observes us on a daily basis, are we concerned that we will hurt him? It is good to have the fear of the Lord, but it is better to respect and love him so much that we don't want to hurt or disappoint Father God by disobeying the will and purpose of our Lord Jesus Christ.

But I will show you whom you should fear: Fear him who, after the killing of the body, has power to throw you into hell.
Luke 12:5

And do not grieve the Holy Spirit of God, with whom you were sealed for the day of redemption.
Ephesians 4:30

Exceptions

Have you ever been tempted to park where there is a clearly posted sign that reads NO PARKING? Have you ever taken advantage of a "Handicapped" parking spot during a rainstorm? When there is a heavy load in your automobile, does convenience override your commitment to other people and the law?

When we park in a restricted area, we must quickly convince ourselves that we are the exception to the NO PARKING sign. For instance, it may be late at night, so we rationalize that the sign doesn't mean all the time. Yet it reads NO PARKING.

Breaking God's laws starts with small things. We convince ourselves that we are the exception to the law, expecting that God will write us into a Book of Exceptions rather than into the Book of Life. Nothing could be further from the truth.

Our own self-centeredness expresses a clear message of disobedience when we go against the simplest rules and laws. Breaking little rules and laws prepares the way for breaking big rules and laws. Conversely, the Scripture says that if we are faithful over the NO PARKING signs of our lives, God will trust us with much.

Whoever can be trusted with very little can also be trusted with much, and whoever is dishonest with very little will also be dishonest with much.
Luke 16:10

Charge It!

Abortion isn't the cause of our problem—it is the result. Our growing national debt that no one wants to pay off, but simply complain about, is not the problem—it is the result. Infrequent Bible reading, spasmodic prayer, and irregular church attendance are not problems—they are results.

Frequently, we look at the result and identify it as the cause of the problem. We need to realize that the cause of our problem is sin, which is alienation from God. Too often, we have a "sin now and pay later" outlook! We are unwilling to deny our human (and fallen) tendencies. We refuse to practice the presence of God by the grace given us in Jesus Christ.

Why be confused about the problem or cause, much less the result? Let's handle the decision at hand, rather than simply saying, "Charge it!"

When we fail to identify and repent for sin, then we put ourselves, our children, our grandchildren, and our great-grandchildren in debt. It makes no difference whether we are speaking of abortion, national debt, or our own extravagances. The cause and the result are the same.

What shall we say, then? Shall we go on sinning so that grace may increase? By no means! We died to sin; how can we live in it any longer?
Romans 6:1-2

Who Are You?

Aristotle says we *are* what we repeatedly *do*. Consider your present actions, thought patterns, spiritual condition, desires, and habits. Then review these against the criteria of repeated activity. Are we truly what we repeatedly do? Can our repeated actions be best described as sinful or full of God's grace? Is there enough evidence in our life to be convicted of being a follower of Jesus?

It was not what Jesus *said* that got him into so much difficulty with the religionists, the state, and the nonbelievers. It was what he *did*. What a difference it would make if each one of us simply served Christ solidly one hour each week! That doesn't mean only worship or Sunday school, but genuinely being Christ *to* someone else. Each of us can change our own world by frequently and repeatedly serving Jesus and our neighbor. We *are* who and what we repeatedly do.

The good man brings good things out of the good stored up in his heart, and the evil man brings evil things out of the evil stored up in his heart. For out of the overflow of his heart his mouth speaks.
Luke 6:45

Faith by itself, if it is not accompanied by action, is dead.
James 2:17

A Christian

A Christian is slow to lose patience and quick to be gracious.

A Christian looks for a way to be constructive and offer a word of encouragement, even when provoked.

A Christian is not a showoff and doesn't try to impress others with self-importance.

A Christian practices good manners and is a living witness to the hospitality of God.

A Christian is not short-tempered or touchy even when insulted or unfairly questioned.

A Christian is a good steward and takes care of the things God has given and also treats others' property with respect.

A Christian thinks the very best, and not the worst, of others.

A Christian does not enjoy another's pain and sin, but is always willing to help and forgive.

But the wisdom that comes from heaven is first of all pure; then peace-loving, considerate, submissive, full of mercy and good fruit, impartial and sincere.
James 3:17

Stunted Growth

Do you wonder why you are not maturing in Jesus Christ? Logical answers might be, "I'm not praying enough, reading the Bible enough, or talking to others about Jesus enough!"

Those all may be true, but they aren't usually basic obstacles to maturing in Christ Jesus. Continued self-hatred for sins of the past will prevent believers from maturing. If you insist on hating yourself for sins that Jesus has already forgiven, you will never mature beyond where you are today.

Let us put behind us those sins that are forgiven and grow in Christ Jesus today.

"Come now, let us reason together,"
says the LORD.
"Though your sins are like scarlet,
they shall be as white as snow;
though they are red as crimson,
they shall be like wool."
Isaiah 1:18

I, even I, am he who blots out
your transgressions, for my own sake,
and remembers your sins no more.
Isaiah 43:25

Family Ties

When Mother Theresa received her Nobel Peace Prize, she was asked, "What can we do to help promote world peace?" "Go home and love your family," was her answer.

Paul writes and tells us,

Wives, submit to your husbands as to the Lord.
Ephesians 5:22

He goes on to say,

Husbands, love your wives, just as Christ loved the church and gave himself up for her.
Ephesians 5:25

Even further, he says,

Children, obey your parents in the Lord, for this is right.
Ephesians 6:1

God is calling us to strong family ties. Faith in God, rooted in family life, has been the source of American success and vitality. As we see America struggling, it is clear that integrity, faith, productivity, respect, and godliness are missing now. These are qualities the Holy Spirit produces in our families.

Let us go home and love our families, because we love the Lord. World peace and national security begin with our care and concern for our families.

God, My Helper

In a news report, Hugh Downs told of a woman who had faked cancer for two years. The woman had cut off her hair and lost thirty pounds in order to make her friends believe she had cancer. She even joined several cancer support groups.

When a health care professional checked her story, it was revealed that the woman was not even physically sick. She had become chronically depressed when her boyfriend broke up with her, so she had decided to garner the sympathy she needed by pretending she was dying.

Where are you getting the attention and support you need? Some turn to money, others turn to misplaced affection. Frequently, people seek worldly support for spiritual needs, but the Scripture is very clear that only the Lord can truly meet our needs. Temporal solutions promote deadly ends. Eternal solutions offer everlasting life.

"Because he loves me," says the LORD, "I will rescue him;
I will protect him, for he acknowledges my name.
He will call upon me, and I will answer him;
I will be with him in trouble,
I will deliver him and honor him.
With long life will I satisfy him and show him my salvation."
Psalm 91:14-16

Where Am I?

In the dead of night a man was walking across a railroad trestle. Suddenly he heard a train coming and had no place to go. Since it was too late to retreat, the man jumped to the side of the bridge and held onto the edge of the trestle. When the train finally passed over him, the man found he didn't have the strength to pull himself up. He was just going to have to hang there. If not, he feared he would fall into the abyss, thousands of feet below.

At daybreak, the man—having hung on for dear life—discovered that he had been hanging only six inches from the ground!

Many people are like the man on the trestle. They perceive that they are in grave danger but don't know exactly where they are. Are you located very close to the Savior? If we remain close to the Lord, we can trust him. He will not let us fall into the abyss.

Seek the LORD while he may be found;
call on him while he is near.
Isaiah 55:6

Heralds

I tell you the truth: Among those born of women there has not risen anyone greater than John the Baptist; yet he who is least in the kingdom of heaven is greater than he.
Matthew 11:11

Do you ever search the Scripture to see exactly what it means? It is very important to read and understand the Word of God precisely. This Scripture makes it clear that if you are a Christian, you are greater than Abraham, King David, King Solomon, and John the Baptist. By Jesus' assessment, John the Baptist outstripped everyone mentioned in the Bible, but the believing Christian is even greater than John the Baptist. John was the greatest at that moment in history because he pointed most clearly to Jesus.

Why does Jesus place such importance on today's believer? Because that believer is pointing the way for redemption and salvation for today's unbeliever. He is opening wide the door of the future for those who will believe in Jesus. Jesus has come and Jesus is coming again. We are to be heralds of this message. *This* is our greatness.

Are you serving Jesus as a herald, a prophet, and a servant believer? In doing this, you become great in the kingdom.

Chocolate Chip—Raspberry Royal

Deciding such matters as which is the best ice cream flavor—chocolate chip, raspberry royal, or plain vanilla—is a question of taste and personal preference, not of truth.

Unfortunately, for many people personal preference is the yardstick of truth. This is unwise, however, because truth stands outside of personal preference. Biblical morality is part of God's objective truth; personal preference is not. Biblical standards of marriage and fidelity are not a matter of personal preference; they are truth. Christian principles in family life, good parenting skills, and the acceptance of responsibility are not matters of personal taste, but divine commandment.

Sometimes personal preference can lead to wrong choices that can deliver us to sin's front door. To walk in God's truth is to prefer him over self. Jesus chose to do the will of the Father and asks us to do likewise.

For I have come down from heaven not to do my will but to do the will of him who sent me.
John 6:38

If anyone chooses to do God's will, he will find out whether my teaching comes from God or whether I speak on my own. He who speaks on his own does so to gain honor for himself, but he who works for the honor of the one who sent him is a man of truth; there is nothing false about him.
John 7:17-18

Chocolate chip or raspberry royal—or even plain vanilla—provide splendid choices, but when we choose the Lord Jesus, preference or taste melts into truth.

Spiritual Vitamins

Mark Twain said, "I can live two months on a single compliment." A pat on the back is only a few vertebrae from a kick in the pants. However, it is certainly miles ahead in encouragement, and it acts as a spiritual vitamin.

When all is said and done, are you a negative person or an affirming one? Have you noticed that many people, when they speak of a friend, employee, associate, or even a relative, do not think of the positive aspects but dwell or focus on the negative?

If you want to be affirmed, then you must affirm others. If you want to be encouraged, you must encourage others. If you want to be spiritually nourished, offer spiritual vitamins to others in the form of affirmations. This isn't false praise. It is offering a godly blessing in a special way.

Jesus put it this way:

Love each other as I have loved you. Greater love has no one than this, that he lay down his life for his friends.
John 15:12-13

Be sure to pass out the spiritual vitamins!

The Magi

Who were those three magi who journeyed to Bethlehem to greet the newborn King?

The magi were priestly scholars and most likely not Jewish, but either Medes or Persians. They were also called "wise men" and "kings."

Each of the presents brought by the magi held special significance. With the gold, they recognized Jesus as king. With the frankincense, they endorsed and bowed before him as high priest. With the myrrh, they announced Jesus' ministry as physician and healer and foretold his death as the sacrifice for the sin of the world.

Their journey to the manger also embodied the surrender of worldly power to Christ's divine spiritual authority. Let us reflect on our worship of King Jesus. To us, is he truly our king, our high priest, our physician and healer, and also the sin sacrifice for us?

Are we willing to journey by faith to him and surrender our worldly power and priorities, placing them under his supreme spiritual authority?

We saw his star in the east and have come to worship him.
Matthew 2:2

Who Has Your Ear?

The Clairol Company has dramatically demonstrated just how powerful advertising is. Just a few years ago, hair coloring for women—not to mention for men—was considered taboo. Only a few nonconforming individuals kept the industry alive. Then copywriter Chirly Poykoff coined the phrase: "Does she, or doesn't she?" Today, four out of ten consumers spend half a billion dollars per year on hair coloring products.

This is a single example of how media can influence our opinions and behavior over a short period of time. Our allegiance depends greatly on who has our ear and what we hear. Where we spend our time and our money makes all the difference in our actions. Beware, be mindful, and be wise.

We have not received the spirit of the world but the Spirit who is from God, that we may understand what God has freely given us. This is what we speak, not in words taught us by human wisdom but in words taught by the Spirit, expressing spiritual truths in spiritual words.
1 Corinthians 2:12-13

Just Stand There?

In seasons like Christmas and Easter, the world offers some very strange wisdom to those who will buy into the program. It goes like this: "Don't just stand there, do something! Buy something! Give something!" But the wisdom of Christ is very different. He says, "Don't just do something, don't just buy something, don't just give something. Stand there!" Stand in the quiet stillness and praise God for his gift of himself, our redemption and infilling.

At these most sacred moments, stand in wonder and in awe of the God who set aside the robes of eternal deity to put on swaddling clothes and lie in a feed trough. Be like the shepherd, the stargazer, the old temple priest named Simeon, who in the midst of a busy world had time to worship, adore, recognize, and celebrate the child Jesus.

We are not only to stand at the foot of the creche, but also at the foot of the cross and worship and praise his name because of who he is, what he has done, what he continues to do—and because we love him.

Forsake worldly wisdom for the very wisdom of God. Stand there—and learn.

For the LORD gives wisdom,
and from his mouth come knowledge and understanding.
Proverbs 2:6

On Guard

We must keep our guard up—to protect ourselves from the world, the flesh, and the devil. Usually the first step in letting one's guard down is to become complacent.

Complacency about the world will cause the believer to wander away from the Lord and slowly begin to agree with and join the world. Complacency about the flesh will cause the believer to seek self-gratification rather than to please the Lord. Complacency about the devil is to forget that there is a spiritual war being waged.

Consider the danger of complacency. During the Gulf War, a Scud missile hit an American army barracks in Saudi Arabia, killing twenty-eight and wounding ninety. Was the Iraqi technology so good that they could pinpoint the place of impact so precisely? No. The Scud missile actually broke apart upon re-entering the atmosphere, and the warhead randomly fell to its deadly destination. The barracks was hit while full of soldiers eating their dinner, who had ignored the air-raid warnings—having become complacent with the American success with the Patriot antimissile technology.

It is easier than you think to become complacent and let your guard down, becoming very vulnerable to the gratification of the flesh, the seduction of the world, and the attack of the devil.

Be self-controlled and alert. Your enemy the devil prowls around like a roaring lion looking for someone to devour.
1 Peter 5:8

What Do You Think of Sin?

How much do you hate sin? How much does it turn you off?

Well, most people can honestly say that some sins turn them off, and other sins turn them on! The sin that we hate in our lives and in others is no problem, but the sin we love might damn us.

There are certain sins that Christians love to hate, such as adultery, drunkenness, gambling, and divorce. But how about the sins of self-righteousness, slander, deception, bitterness, and malice?

The Lord Jesus knew before the foundation of the world every thought and action that we would have, and he loves us just the same. But he has called us to hate the sin that separates us from him.

Jesus replied, "I tell you the truth, everyone who sins is a slave to sin."
John 8:34

For the wages of sin is death, but the gift of God is eternal life in Christ Jesus our Lord.
Romans 6:23

Playing Hurt

In professional sports the athletes often continue to play even when hurt. Frequently you see them with taped legs, hands, or protective devices on their wrists or forearms. Roger Staubach, a very famous quarterback for the Dallas Cowboys for many years, made this comment: "If you are not playing hurt, you are not really playing."

The most hurtful fact in all of history is the crucifixion of Jesus. On his way to the cross, he lived a life of rejection and was totally misunderstood. He was beaten, spat upon, and bore sins that were not his. It almost seems too flippant to say, "He played hurt."

Why is it that we sometimes feel that we are going to make it through this sinful world unscathed? How silly it is to believe that we will have no suffering. C. S. Lewis said, "God *whispers* to us in our well-being. God *shouts* to us in our suffering."

Does it take suffering to make us appreciate blessing? And must we face death before understanding life?

Endure hardship as discipline; God is treating you as sons. For what son is not disciplined by his father? ... No discipline seems pleasant at the time, but painful. Later on, however, it produces a harvest of righteousness and peace for those who have been trained by it.
Hebrews 12:7, 11

I'm playing hurt. So did Jesus. He won . . . and so will we.

Personal Trust

A story ran in the *Cleveland Plain Dealer* about a Toyota automobile manufacturing plant in Georgetown, Kentucky. A Mr. Cho manages the plant of thirty-five-hundred employees. At this particular plant, not one employee has ever been laid off. Actually, they are not called "employees"; they are called "team workers" or "team members."

Mr. Cho wears blue jeans, tennis shoes, and a short-sleeved shirt as he works with his team workers. Mr. Cho renews a pledge every six months that he puts in writing which says, "Before there is one employee laid off, there will be deep salary cuts for every executive." This is a very different situation than what is found in American manufacturing plants, where sometimes thousands are laid off from work.

The average employee at the Georgetown plant earns $14 per hour, while at a comparable General Motors plant, the employees average $35 per hour. At the Toyota plant, you can't find a person who will criticize the management or the working conditions. What a difference trust makes in personal production and individual attitudes!

Love is made complete among us so that we will have confidence on the day of judgment, because in this world we are like him. There is no fear in love. But perfect love drives out fear, because fear has to do with punishment.
1 John 4:17-18

When we draw close to Jesus, our fear is dispelled. Confidence is our attitude, and productivity is the result.

Rewards?

A young man on his way home from school found two canvas sacks lying in the street. Upon inspecting them, he was amazed to see that the sacks were full of money—a total of $415,000. He returned the money to the Princeton Armored Service and received a $1,000 reward.

The young man was unhappy and said that he had expected a much larger reward. In fact, upon being interviewed, he said, "I don't understand it." He complained, "If I had it to do over again, I would probably keep the money." He had returned the money merely to get a reward.

Sometimes we're like that young man. Are you and I living the Christian life for an immediate reward or possibly just to avoid the shame and guilt of sin? Jesus wants us to live our Christian life because we love him with all of our heart, soul, and mind. To be simply obeying the law to avoid the consequences is to live in fear. Likewise, to be living the Christian life just for the reward is to miss the wonderful privilege of living for Jesus because of our real love for him.

Let love and faithfulness never leave you;
bind them around your neck,
write them on the tablet of your heart.
Then you will win favor and a good name
in the sight of God and man.
Proverbs 3:3-4

Super Glue

Recently I was using Super Glue, and my finger became glued to the object. It struck me at that moment how our words can "Super Glue" things to people. For example, while I was visiting in a home one day, the parent introduced one of their children to me, saying, "This is Sally, the slow one."

When another child entered the room, the parent said, "This is Johnny, the clumsy one."

I don't believe that parent, or any of us, realizes how such words hurt a child. No matter what the situation, whether it be an inherent problem or a sin, we can inextricably glue problems to people with our words.

Had I tried to pull my finger away from the object to which it was attached, it would have torn my flesh. It reminded me that we simply can't tear away things that have been said to us. To properly detach my finger from the object, I had to pour on acetone. Instantly, this solvent freed me.

Would you like to be freed from hurt, devaluation, depression, and loneliness? Then use the solvent of the Holy Spirit. He can set you free when all the tearing, thrashing, and good intentions to be set free can only do further damage. He can even take away the hurtful words.

The Holy Spirit is God's solvent and our freedom.

It is for freedom that Christ has set us free. Stand firm, then, and do not let yourselves be burdened again by a yoke of slavery.
Galatians 5:1

Life's Success Formula

I tried + I failed + I trusted = He succeeded!

There are so many pastoral and personal problems among the people of God that do not need to exist. The greatest counselor I know is the Holy Spirit, who speaks to us as we meditate on the Word of God. By hearing, receiving, and living the Word of God, the issues of life become simplified and very solvable.

If you have *tried* and perhaps *failed*, begin to *trust* and watch Jesus *succeed* in your life.

In all my prayers for all of you, I always pray with joy because of your partnership in the gospel from the first day until now, being confident of this, that he who began a good work in you will carry it on to completion until the day of Christ Jesus.
Philippians 1:4-6

Yet I am not ashamed, because I know whom I have believed, and am convinced that he is able to guard what I have entrusted to him for that day.
2 Timothy 1:12

Just Say No

If Satan can make us truly lazy by a spirit of slothfulness that would destroy our lives, likewise he could make us so truly overactive that he could destroy our lives with "busyness." Jesus wants us to discern when to say yes, and when to say no. Quite frankly, he wants us to say no more often than probably many of us do.

Followers of Jesus realize that the devil continually prowls this earth seeking to destroy God's people. Many feel that they cannot take a break and must work without ceasing. The evil one would like to badger you into overwork. Just because the devil never takes vacations doesn't mean that the righteous shouldn't take a Sabbath rest. From time to time Jesus withdrew, and he said, "Come with me by yourselves to a quiet place and get some rest" (Mark 6:31).

There is so much to do and so many wonderful things to be accomplished for the Lord. There are church and family demands, personal and professional demands. The need is great; but the same Lord who told us to labor six days tells us to rest one day. *It is a matter of balance.*

Remember the Sabbath day by keeping it holy. Six days you shall labor and do all your work, but the seventh day is a Sabbath to the LORD your God.
Exodus 20:8-10

By relaxing in Jesus—by spending Sabbath time with him—his holiness can become ours. And we can destroy the works of Satan in our lives.

Serendipity

Have you ever received a letter from the Internal Revenue Service with an unexpected refund check? That's serendipity!

Have you been shopping and fallen in love with an item that you just knew was far beyond your budget and found that it was marked down fifty percent? That's serendipity!

Did you ever agree to do a favor for a friend and go on a blind date—and find that your date is a beautiful or handsome, wonderful, marvelous person who fulfills your wildest dreams? That's serendipity!

Another way to spell *serendipity* is g-r-a-c-e. Grace is God's way of surprising us with his blessed presence and glorious benefits.

Grace and peace to you from God our Father and the Lord Jesus Christ.
Philippians 1:2

This is how you understand true serendipity. Where is God's grace touching you?

Have You Spanked Your Child Lately?

God believes in spanking, and so do I.

Sin and judgment are facts of life for everyone. The wages of sin for children of all ages is exactly the same: death. It is the duty of parents, spiritual authorities, workers, and corporate executives alike to say "no" to sin and "yes" to righteousness.

Youngsters must be taught at the earliest age that reconciliation is the most wonderful answer. Spanking must not be associated with anger, pain, and rejection, but with love and a pathway to reconciliation.

He who spares the rod hates his son,
but he who loves him is careful to discipline him.
Proverbs 13:24

Discipline on all levels must be full of care. The ministering of a spanking should be carefully done in peace, not retaliation. It should sting but must never cause damage.

Have you noticed that as children get older, a spanking takes different forms? It may be a grounding or a suspension of a privilege, or the loss of an opportunity.

Spanking and hugging are opposite sides of the same coin, which is God's love.

Reflections can also sting.

In John Doe We Trust

How did a nation of people who carry currency that states, "In God We Trust," get to be so trusting in ourselves that we can eliminate God?

Modern education is dominated by a cold naturalism and a shallow humanism that are enemies of personal faith. Often God's greatest blessings are explained away as natural phenomena or the expressions of human achievement. Courses in science and literature dismiss true religion, and psychology often treats spiritual commitment as a psychic aberration.

G. K. Chesterton observed, "Not that man will believe in nothing, but that he will believe in anything." And we see that happening. Scripture says that there is only one true and perfect God experienced in Father, Son, and Holy Spirit. Course studies can be no match for divine revelation, which we experience in our mind, heart, and even in our environment.

God speaks his nature through his creation and yet lovingly stands beyond it. To know Christ Jesus is to know oneself and to love self and others. To know Christ Jesus is to trust in God and not John Doe, John Doe's teacher, or what John Doe knows or believes.

Trust in the LORD forever,
for the LORD, the LORD, is the Rock eternal.
Isaiah 26:4

Encourage One Another

You're Beautiful—Great Job—My Friend—You're Special—*You're a Blessing*—**Way to Play**—Way to Work—**Well Done**—You're Unique—*How Smart of You*—Awesome—Great Job—Fantastic—*Best Ever*—You're So Sensitive—You're a Winner—Way to Start—Great Finish—Uh Huh—*I Admire You*—**Good Going**—Looking Great—Way to Finish—You're Spectacular—*Now You're Cooking*—**I Really Respect You**—*You Mean Everything to Me*—Thanks for Being Just You—*What a Witness*—*So Special*—**You're Cool**—Thanks—*God Bless*—**Jesus Shines Through You**—What a Friend—You're the Greatest—*How Creative*—**You're a Real Problem Solver**—You're Right—You're Dead Center—**You're Faithful**—You're Obedient—How Loving—**Thanks for the Truth**—You're Number One—Thanks for the Help—**I Need You**—*You're Precious*—Hi, Friend—*You're God's Person*—**I See Jesus in You**—I Love You—Buddy—*You're Mine*—**How Brave**—You're on the Way—**You Don't Give Up**—*You're Big Time*—Now You're Rolling—You Care—**Love You**—How Smart—**That's Neat!**

But encourage one another daily, as long as it is called Today, so that none of you may be hardened by sin's deceitfulness.
Hebrews 3:13

The Next Five Miles

About 350 years ago, a shipload of pioneers landed on the northeast coast of America. The first year they established a town site; the next year, the town government planned to build a road five miles west into the wilderness. During the fourth year, the people tried to impeach the town government because they thought it was a waste of public funds to build a road five miles westward into a wilderness. After all, who needed to go *there*, anyway?

This is a picture of the people who had the vision to see across three thousand miles of ocean and overcame great hardships to complete the vision. But in just a few years, they were not able to see even five miles out of town. They had lost the vision and their pioneering courage.

St. Paul's words are very clear as he addresses the issue of vision and courage:

So then, King Agrippa, I was not disobedient to the vision from heaven.
Acts 26:19

To deny the vision from heaven for each of us is to lose our way. For with clear vision of what we can become in Christ Jesus, no ocean of difficulty is too great, no road of adversity too long, nor any mountain of perseverance too high for those called according to God's purposes. However, without vision and the presence of Jesus in our lives and the power of the Holy Spirit, we can hardly move beyond our current boundaries, whether it be in our family, school, career, business, or church, not to mention five miles out of town.

Out in the Open

Whether we like it or not, in this society things are out in the open. It makes no difference whether you are marketing pornographic books or operating an abortion clinic. As taxpayers, we paid a multi-million-dollar bill to have literature on AIDS mailed into every home in this country. Condoms are an everyday topic, and homosexuality is an everyday reality and part of the political scenario.

A serious misunderstanding is what really stands in the way of America's experiencing a great restoration and being God's light in a dark world. Many people believe that it is the democratic system, spurred either by the Democrats or the Republicans, that has made this country great. Yet, in world history, no government has ever met all the needs of the people, or has successfully been the protector and provider of any given society.

Only when there has been a strong demonstration of the power of God and a commitment to his purposes has any society succeeded. America's great contributions to the world are related to her early love for the Lord God and our Savior, Jesus Christ. It was open and uncompromised commitment to him that brought blessing to our country's foundations.

I ask you to return to the faith of those who came to our shores in the earliest stages. Witness to what the Lord is doing in your life, in order that America may continue to be a shining light in a dark world. To remain silent and leave it to government is to sign this country's death certificate. Let us "go public" with Jesus!

Let your light shine before men, that they may see your good deeds and praise your Father in heaven.
Matthew 5:16

Index of Scripture Passages

Index of Subjects